FELLOWSHIP

FELLOWSHIP

Darren J. Nash

Fellowship
By Darren J. Nash

Grateful acknowledgement is made to Dr Leo K. K. Wong, Professor Richard Yu, and Darren J. Nash for permission to reprint the images in this book.

ISBN: 978-988-237-012-8

The Chinese University Press
The Chinese University of Hong Kong
Sha Tin, N.T., Hong Kong
Fax: +852 2603 7355
E-mail: cup@cuhk.edu.hk
Website: www.chineseupress.com

Printed in Hong Kong

To Olivia & Isobel

Contents

Author's Preface

This collection was born out of the author having a terrible memory! Having spent almost 25 years supporting research in clinical medicine I struggled, and still do, to retain even a small understanding of the inspirational work of my colleagues. Many Professors, researchers, students, doctors and nurses have been generous with their time and patience in attempting to improve my understanding of what they are researching. What started out as some very short mnemonic pieces to aid recall has grown into this collection.

My hope is that these eclectic pieces and their stylistic range reflect the diversity of research in the field of medicine. The topics examined range from health economics and specific diseases to biological mechanisms and technology platforms used in research. Some also provide a lens to the feelings and pressures of patients and doctors, whilst others delve into the workings of the mind. Several have layers and patterns for the reader to discover as an allusion to the process of research itself, whilst others are painfully personal in the perspectives they use. The images in the collection offer respite for the reader from poems which often have turmoil at their heart, a chance to take a breath and be reminded of the beauty that surrounds us.

It starts with the key to successful research; collaboration and fellowship, and ends on a reflection of humanity and the humbling of mankind gained through service to others. As such the collection epitomises the path that transforms passion into perfection, and enshrines the drive of the Faculty of Medicine at The Chinese University of Hong Kong to gain and apply knowledge and understanding for the benefit of all.

We should never skip to the last page of a book and read the ending. However in this case I think it is apt, so I shall borrow from the last line of the collection in the hope it conveys the honour I feel in making this contribution.

'I leave this token at your door, humbled.'

Darren J. Nash

Foreword by the Vice-Chancellor

We are 35!

The young Faculty of Medicine at CUHK has reached 35 years! This is a long and amazing journey rooted from the visionary leadership of Professor Gerald Choa and the torch passed to the youngest Dean, Professor Francis Chan.

Success has never been easy but its fruit taste better by chewing on the challenges we faced and the support we obtained along the way. Memories revive from teaching in a cargo box to the most sophisticated laboratories and lecture theatres, from no more than 40 MBChB students to a cohort of 235 each year, and from many stories of breakthroughs in research and innovations leading us to the top 50 medical school in the world. No words can sufficiently express our gratitude to the contributions of founding professors and teachers which built the departments and programs from scratch, to colleagues in the medical professions including the Academy of Medicine, and various Colleges as well as international collaborators. Without their staunch support, this small child can never grow up to his full strength.

On this special occasion of 35th anniversary, our happiness is augmented by Mr Darren Nash of the Nuffield Department of Medicine who contributed his beautiful poems that sing the four seasons of life. Through these words, we reflect upon life and death, meditate through pain and joy, ponder on diseases and remedies. I would also like to thank the two great masters of photography, Professor Richard Yu and Dr Leo Wong, for their generosity of sharing beautiful pictures to color these poems. Through their eyes and skillful use of cameras, aqua and snow, blossom and fruits, birds and clouds whisper the meaning of life and Mother Nature.

May I wish the Faculty of Medicine continue to flourish in science and discoveries. May I call upon all colleagues and students to uphold professionalism and humanity. May I join the jubilation of the first 35 years of amazing success and many more years to come.

Joseph Sung

Foreword by the Dean of the Faculty of Medicine

I am grateful beyond words for the boundless generosity of Mr Darren Nash to permit us to publish his poems in celebration of the 35th anniversary of the Faculty of Medicine of The Chinese University of Hong Kong (CUHK). It is our great honour and privilege to have received treasured birthday gifts—photos from Dr Leo Wong and Professor Richard Yu. This book of poems with photos from two renowned Hong Kong contemporary photographers in the medical profession will help you see the world of medicine in more concrete and profound perspectives. You will discover for yourself in their artistic creations, an infusion of broad perspectives and concerns about the society and the human conditions such as uncertainty, fear, hope, dying and aging.

Time and time again I have been asked how to educate competent, caring physicians to meet societal expectations of healthcare. Medicine is the science and art of healing. Good doctors play verbal acrobatics to cajole patients to change lifestyle or to adhere to a medication regimen for improved outcomes. Artistic creations, a powerful form of communicating feelings, can open eyes and minds of individuals to see the world differently, a world of possibilities. It is the cross-fertilization of science and art that intellectual wholeness is to be attained. The Faculty is committed to inculcating this wholeness in our students to enable them to see medicine and professionalism beyond the boundary of expertise, embracing a vista that includes perspectives in broad social contexts.

The Faculty is most grateful for having received these 35th birthday gifts from our fellowship, which is the title of this book of poems. Your unstinting support and encouragement have enabled us to course the path of the past 35 years with many remarkable and memorable success stories. We will continue to count on your unconditional love and solidarity to meet challenges in the years ahead.

Lastly, I would like to also devote this book to our unsung heroes, whose patience and support over three and a half decades have been crucial to our success. They are our loved ones who have to put up with our absence in gatherings and the deadlines as our profession puts the benefits of patients above our own.

At 35, mature and agile, the Faculty of Medicine of CUHK has transformed a lot of experience into valuable insights. These insights will continue to guide us to be a part of the solution in the arena of medicine, health sciences and healthcare delivery.

Francis K. L. Chan

Photography Contributors

Dr Leo K. K. Wong

MBBS (HK), FRCP (London, Edinburgh, Glasgow), FHKCP
Hon FRPS, Hon PSA, FPSA, MPSA, Hon EFIAP, MFIAP, Hon FPSHK

Graduated from The University of Hong Kong in 1959, Dr Leo Wong received and completed his clinical training in the Government Medical Unit in Kowloon Hospital (1960–1962) and Princess Margaret Hospital (1963–1965) under Dr K. C. Tsang. He was seconded to UMU in Queen Mary Hospital in 1961–1962. He was sent by the Hong Kong Government to Glasgow Royal Infirmary for one year (1964–1965) for training under Professor A. S. Douglas. Returning to Hong Kong in 1966, he served as Senior Medical Officer in Medical Unit C in Princess Margaret Hospital. He went into private practice in 1971 and retired in 2006.

Photography is Dr Wong's lifelong passion and love. He studied Photography under master photographer SF DAN in 1966. Since 2005, he has held over 50 photographic exhibitions of which 40 were in Hong Kong and Mainland China and about 10 overseas in Paris, Switzerland, San Francisco, Benin, Taipei, Bangkok, Kuala Lumpur, Singapore and Macau. His works are collected by museums and art lovers. Dr Wong has published over 10 photographic albums, the latest being "Ode to the seasons."

In July 2010, he was awarded the Bronze Bauhinia Star (BBS) by the HKSAR Government for his achievement in photographic art and his exemplary efforts in promoting the development of photographic art in Hong Kong, the mainland and overseas.

Dr Wong is currently Honorary Advisor to the China Photographers Association, Museum Expert Advisor to the Leisure and Cultural Services Department, and Honorary President of the Photographic Society of Hong Kong and Photographic Salon Exhibitors Association.

Professor Richard Y. H. Yu

MD (HK), PhD (London), FRCP (London, Edinburgh, Glasgow), FRACP (Hon), FHKCP, FHKAM (Medicine), FAMS, Hon FRCPS (Glasgow), Hon FHKCP, DSocSc (Hon) (HK), Hon DSSc (CUHK), Hon FPSHK

Professor Richard Yu is currently Honorary Professor of the Department of Medicine at The University of Hong Kong, Department of Medicine & Therapeutics at The Chinese University of Hong Kong, and Honorary Consultant Physician at the Ruttonjee and Princess Margaret Hospitals. After graduating from The University of Hong Kong (1958), he completed his clinical training in the Government Medical Unit under Dr Gerald Choa in Queen Mary Hospital and research at the University College Hospital, London where he was awarded a Ph.D in 1966. He then held the posts of Lecturer and Senior Lecturer in the Department of Medicine, The University of Hong Kong where he was awarded the MD before going into private practice (1973), but continues to teach in the Department as Honorary Clinical Lecturer, Honorary Clinical Associate Professor and later Honorary Clinical Professor.

Professor Yu holds Fellowships of the Colleges of Physicians in Hong Kong, UK and Australia; and of the Academies of Medicine of Hong Kong and Singapore and Honorary doctorates in Social Science from both universities. He was the Founding Honorary Secretary of the Hong Kong College of Physicians (1986–1995), then Vice-President for Education (1993–1995) and later served as President from 1998 to October 2004. As the Past President and ex-official and Senior Advisor (2010) in the Council, he continues to contribute to the College in an advisory capacity.

He is the founding member of the Society of Nephrology and the Hong Kong Kidney Foundation in 1979 serving as Honorary Treasurer and Board Member respectively. The Society has elected him as Honorary Advisor and he is a Patron of the Foundation.

Darren J. Nash

Darren J. Nash holds an MBA from the University of Oxford, and a BSc (Hons) from Oxford Brookes University. He has supported medical research for almost 25 years at the University of Oxford. He is the Associate Head of the Nuffield Department of Medicine at the University of Oxford, and a Director of three university subsidiary companies. This support has been at a global level as he is responsible for research infrastructures not only in the UK but also in China, Africa, South East Asia and Latin America. For the past decade, he has been successfully supporting and developing collaborative research in Hong Kong and across China.

His experiences in medical research have led to the creation of poetry as an 'aide memoir' as he admits to having a terrible memory and used poetry as a mechanism to remember the science his colleagues have attempted to educate him about in the past 25 years. He remains grateful for their patience.

He lives and works in Oxford. This is his first published poetry collection.

Photograph by Leo K. K. Wong.

POEMS

Fellowship

I argued with the sea for a while,
but it needed no sentry, so I led down.

I sought comfort from the earth for a while,
but it did not take me in, so I stood up.

I berated the sky for a while,
but it heeded no plea, so I turned inward.

I focused my mind for a while,
but it held no answers, so I gave up.

I leant into the wind for a while,
but it offered no support, so I was alone.

I fed a witless fire for a while,
but it burnt my hands, so I sought aid.

I joined hands with my fellows,
and found the succour I sought.

I should have known.

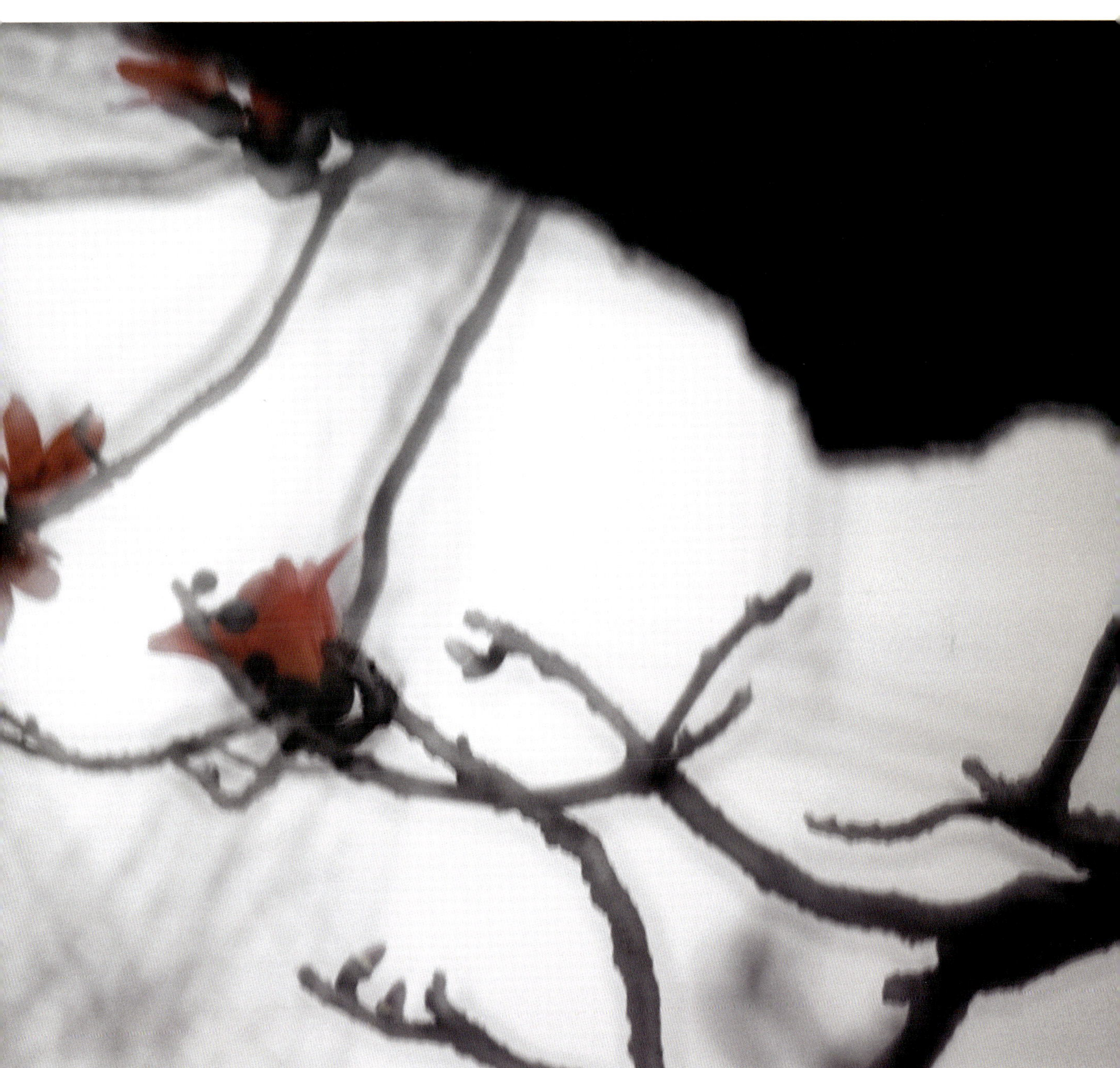

Photograph by Richard Yu.

Photograph by Darren J. Nash.

The Beastly Economics of Prescriptions

a sonic nomic zips right by.
Of eco genus? Know not I.

a manic panic stopped me still.
All efficacious? That's the pill.

a neuron firing fed the light.
Things comprehended? What a sight.

a Turing person adds it through.
Keeping up? Now added true.

hand it over there's a love.
A tenner please! Oh Lords above.

no market beta, no risk explained.
My pockets empty! expression pained.

Photograph by Leo K. K. Wong.

Moving Forward

I think not.
It really does not work.
To move forward,
place one foot in front of another.
Not in your mouth.

I think so.
It has the capacity to disrupt.
To move forward,
engage you brain before you talk.
Lest your mouth run away with your feet.

I think perhaps.
It has an unfortunate consequence.
To move forward,
pray to win the ear of hope.
Talk as if you have brains.

I think indeed.
It is true.
To move forward,
sharpen your elbows and let them speak
against those who would not queue.

Photograph by Darren J. Nash.

Tourmaline Pole Apocalypse

dum′
Scarlet shadows on faded horizons
Mortured trees on poisons edge
Jaded visions fatal end-point
Life I've Negated
Respite of Pressure
Life I've Posited
Alizarin freshet stirs nativity
Growan flowers cognate seed
Orche cadence of dawning futures
.mud

Doubting Thomas

Lost I am upon this earth,
sight darkened by much dread,
a blindness that terrifies and stifles me,
and locks me in my head.

Yet terrified I look about,
oracular in vision,
a sense of certainty abides within,
and so I form decision.

A resonance of warmth unfolds,
as awaken I from sleep,
emerging thus to look around,
at what is mine to keep.

Assurance floods my consciousness,
the third eye's vision kept.
The warmth I sought surrounded me,
as in your shoulder I wept.

No charm required no stone to turn,
for brightness fills my life.

A fool I am for doubting thus,
for love is simply life.

Photograph by Darren J. Nash.

Exculpation

Keep to my bed, take your medicine you said.
This ha-ha that keeps the living from the dead,
messes with my head.

Keep to my bed, be a good boy you said.
This bourne hems me in so I barely see kin,
gaining but blistering skin.

Keep to my bed, to avoid infection you said.
This sty you teach me confines my soul,
yet recovery is still the goal?

Keep to my bed, take more medicine you said.
This stutting keeps the Devil from my door,
regard my ever wan pallor.

Keep to my bed, be a brave boy you said.
This wain I seek eludes me still,
no strength to surmount this life's hill.

Keep to my bed, don't infect others you said.
This buboed life is fierce and fell,
harken to the loudening knell.

Ah ha, the ditch is crossed, the boundary is no more,
the path is clear, the support is gone,
the savaged life gains deaths only advantage.

Photograph by Darren J. Nash.

Photograph by Richard Yu.

Aid Me

My cousin gave me a favour, now lost in time,
seeking origins may serve up a remedy.

My father the ill gourmand, sought sustenance,
bad habits died out before we did.

My mother fed her children, as all mothers do,
her own fate transmitted irrevocably.

My brothers and my sisters continue to search,
dusk has not yet settled, so hope is alive.

My friends give generously, still only protection exists,
the favour continues to change.

My God has a reason, succour is still sought,
but an occluded purpose shakes faith.

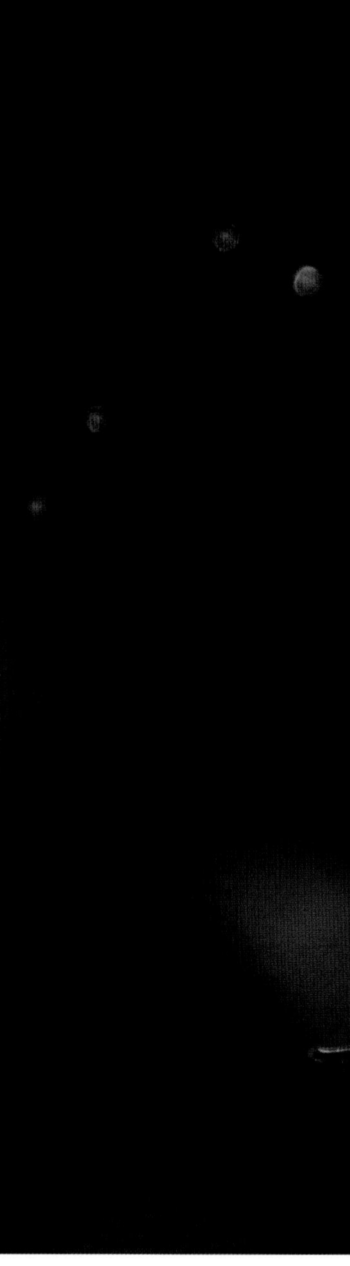

Photograph by Richard Yu.

Photograph by Darren J. Nash.

Cradle

Arid not fecund, small hope of seeded joy,
inward turning mind, self-destructive ploy.
Shocked, his grace of favours, risen me from deep,
enrapture my whole being, breathless I do weep.

Florid and petulant, no dulcet tones just ire,
ravening my ear drums, until all breath does expire.
Shocked, her gaze of saucers, their depths to which I fall,
ensorcell my whole being, removing all screams pall.

Solid and replete, no site of meted love,
outward facing future, generosity from above.
Shocked, his snap of fingers, a rapid fall from grace,
enraged my whole being, no future can I face.

Turbid and moribund, no legacy shall I leave,
fracturing my sanity, undoing my minds weave.
Shocked, the spiral deepens, no succour can be found,
enshroud my whole being, and place it in the ground.

*Rem*ember the way

Caught not by the flocks that pass by my eyes,
I stared through the ceiling and onto the skies.
Released not to the slumber so vainly sought.
Childhood lessons so vainly taught.
Axis turns.
Day becomes night and still sleep has no sway,
If only my mind could remember the way.
Alpha not Delta so to drugs I do stoop.
Night becomes day my eyelids do droop.

Ångström

Beyond bright you burn to resolve the truth,
a million million suns yet only now can I see.
You show me your faces, but I need more.
Even cloned your expression is the same,
to your domain I must travel.
If I am to conserve your beauty, I must unravel.
Motifs beckon and hint, but to what purpose?
Every crease and furrow, every fold and pocket
lends you meaning, and directs my attention.
Conformation, confirmation, cure.

Photograph by Darren J. Nash.

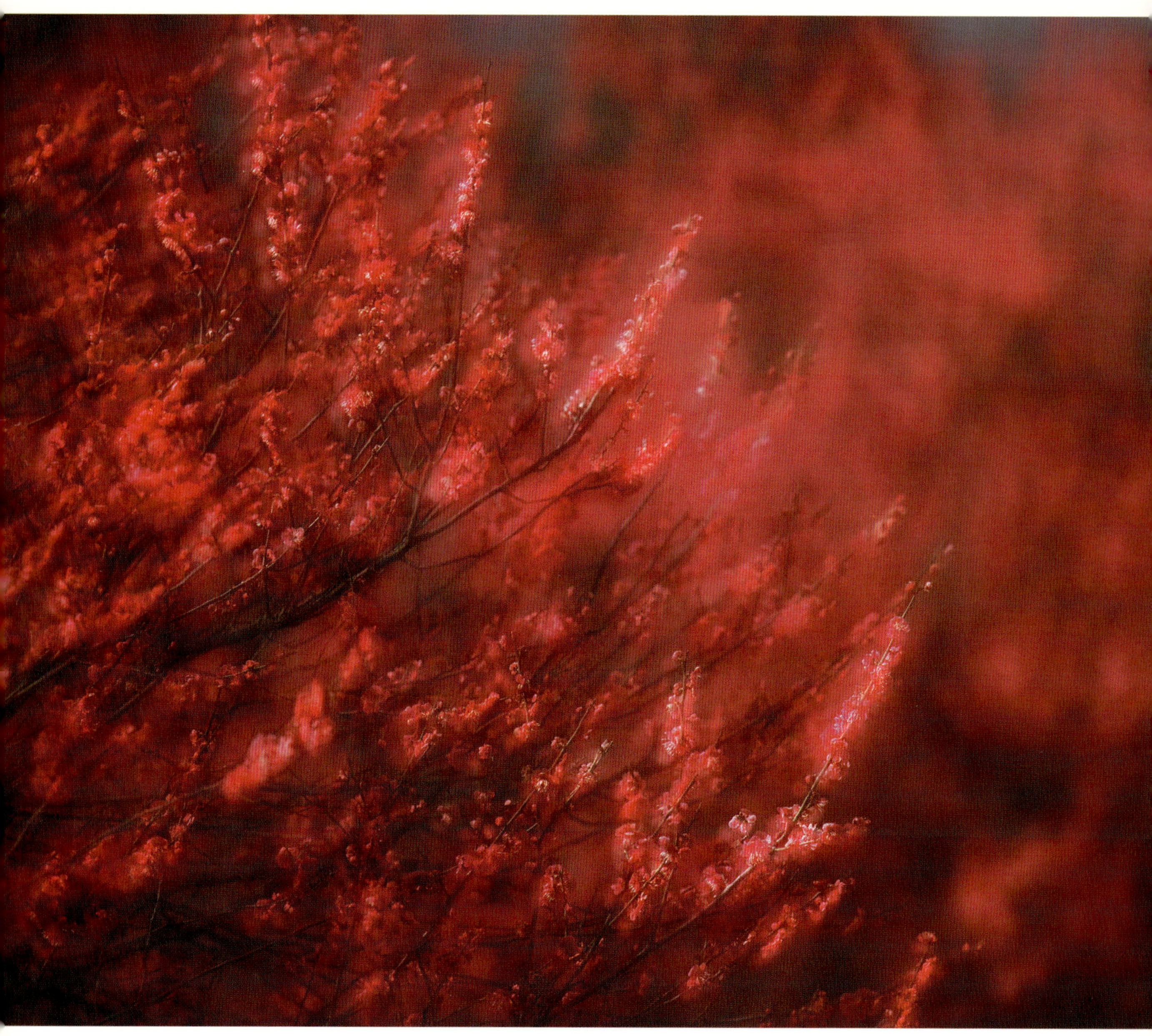

Photograph by Leo K. K. Wong.

Fractionally Inspired

Perfusion rides a merry-go-round,
pressure waxing and waning,
passive gradients aspired to.
Alveolus and her sisters intercede,
diffusing the moment,
they use the ferric blade.
I am pale still,
but not so blue.
Concentration avoids the one-way ticket.

Nod2

A cursory nod or two pays no dividends.
The Crone despises the lack of even handedness that created her.
She blames some cruel act of my divinity.
As the drip slows
she-fishes more urgently amongst the clagging reeds of her being,
she'd be better off left in the wild.

Photograph by Leo K. K. Wong.

Photograph by Darren J. Nash.

To Rose Inn

Rest I on no laurels, ore in tons we shall find!
Yet one is torn, re notions of wealth may abide in others too.
We should stop re tis noon past; to Rose Inn we shall hurry.
To yon ironstone tor we must orient, son, pass my reins onto me.
No stonier ground than my mind can be found.

§

I will not for an eon sit, nor will I wait longer still, rent I soon a room?
Care I not one snit or jot for your tone sir no! I put no store in your words.
But o' risen not to ire am I, simply to forestall neon riots in my head.
Snort I one pinch of snuff whilst you consider that my heart is like stone,
iron is my will, my companions, nine, roost here for the evening I say!

§

My mouth I must rinse, onto the bar, odd that none sit or dine here.
This food is roe in snot! Is this the standard I set? No, nor do I accept it,
Also she sings no sonnet I have ever heard, I am noise torn!
I would rather put mine nose in rot, or rub mine eyes with onion,
rest assured, you will move this siren onto some other task!

§

Partners, in ten or so minutes I will to bed, inert soon I shall be.
I am not senior of age but there is no relief of tension or respite offered.
To bed, and snore I not, not one stir, no, not the whole night through.
I do by rote sin on, skyward even Orion's net finds not the bounty I hunt.
For my inner soot marks me a sinner too, and clouds sleep from my sight.

Photograph by Darren J. Nash.

Photograph by Richard Yu.

Immolation

A grain of restive notion wends its way to meaning.
Vainly it seeks reason.

No guide nor totem can it find to aid its coalescence into reality.
Failure raising neither fume nor fury.

It persists refusing unborn defeat.
Notion seeks to adorn itself in character.

Ilks conclave lends succour and grants maturities dress.
Resolution is born.

Now erudite in stride its surge educates the growing pupil.
Flushed with achievement it is fulfilled in the conflagration of action.

Would That

Would that I could find a charm to lighten this lack-lustre world,
but in this world charm is forsaken for irreverence,
and lost in darkness it brightly burns as spite.

Would that a spirit could lift me, of a warm and gentle nature,
but in this world nature's spirit of gentility is ridiculed,
and descending still — a coldness steels our hearts.

Would that we could mend our hurts to bring about a thaw,
but in this world Thor's hurts are reconciled with war,
and broken are those who try to heal.

Would that all had grace to kneel afore the splendour bright,
but in this world our brightest ken'll ne'er harken to his sight,
and standing awkward pride bars our way.

Would that faith could find a way to materialise its presence,
but in this world no prescience liaises with this reality,
and miracles are not a mortal's gift.

Photograph by Darren J. Nash.

Photograph by Leo K. K. Wong.

Listen

I wish you were blind.
So the tears of my eyes
wouldn't blind you with pity.

I wish you were deaf.
So the rattle of my lungs
wouldn't deafen your mind.

I wish you were dumb,
so the lies of my tongue
wouldn't numb you with inaction.

I wish you would go,
so the pain of my being
wouldn't torture your soul.

I wish all sorts of things.
Just listen.
Hear me.
Now.

I wish you wouldn't love me
So what's left of your life
would be filled with joy.

Photograph by Leo K. K. Wong.

Bade

Uncloaked by the dawn
faithless are the shadows of the morn.
Now harried by the light, a flight of steps awakens
and is handmaiden from earth to air.
In kind gesture to the day to come
a halo bade me smile, spinning flaxen to gold.
Daily is born this gift from the light,
then borne away in glaring site.
Starkly lived,
a grace of boughs thoughtful susurrus bade me sit awhile,
awaiting the day to be undone.
As I mourn my cloak,
the hand that accepts no tarry on the stair will soon beckon.

Buckle

Raked fast and furious
Beggared belief abounded
Yet the runnels of blood
gave credence to the sight

Fistful's of air punched
Handfuls of hair scrunched
Vision occluded by ire's veil
Null rapture unseen

Welts rising to the surface
Aggressions map made real
Journey adorned by wrath
The lived in suit crumpled

The brakes of temperance failed
Field of screams harvested
Crop of broken bones
Craw of savoured pheromones

Buckled to the bed now
Staple fed the cure-all
Arc of current crackles
Torrent burns and blisters

Vapid giggle bubbles
Spat at for my troubles
Splint for soul and body
and I am the sane one?

Photograph by Richard Yu.

Witless Precession

Gaia let me down, she uncrowned me.
For I was too great a burden.
Though the cunning woman had left her
pontil mark bare across my skin,
I am now as unmade.

Oh I am of her substance still,
though I am no longer made man,
a golem and without inheritance.
A poppet if you will, of cloth and sticks,
hungry for life.

I know it is her, burdened with millennium old ardour
her sex still stands proud, as church to the penitent,
as geography to the traveller.
Her once children seek them out,
craving the succour of her beauty within and without,
blind to the travesty of the destruction they wreck.

Photograph by Leo K. K. Wong.

She would deny us such things,
but even cast adrift our frame of time
is an argot too swift for her old bones.
Be not fooled, her dominion is un-diminished,
Her emotions born change her white skirts of fancy
to an indiscriminate dervish, tearing a path through lost humanity.

Transported by enragement she believes our germ line is moribund.
Perhaps her ley neurology has degraded.
She no longer tilts her smile in our direction,
her seasons of wit are gone.

Photograph by Leo K. K. Wong.

Crooked Path

The wooden post was cracked as was the paint upon it.
A hinge with no gate in sight, at least to me;
indecision reigns, around and through it.
The path was clear yet overgrown with doubt,
pebbled with patches of make-good; skin of my thoughts.
Its destination of unknown futures beckoning.
Hobbled by stitch and itched by stubble,
more afoot than my lace less and faithless shoe.
Fate pinching me like my ingrown toenail.
Move, move.

If only Pan or Hamlyn would provide encouragement.
Dirge or dire whisper I care not which now.
I need more than a casual beckon, nee a clarion for these lugs.
The carrion on my bones holds no attraction,
the skin of these thoughts now dressed in the habit of doubt.
This map of sagacity, no tale of two towers;
getting nowhere on these torn tickets to the sky.
Anchored to the earth in some profane and errant truth,
not daring to trim the hangnail that pesters.
Faithless, faithless.

What was I about, turn and turn again.
My obstinate gaze sees little, hooded by more than flesh.
Hogweed creases those hoods now, vented to sinus,
acerbic and witless.

Photograph by Richard Yu.

It makes me suck a whistled breath, chilling my face as
these less than thoughts speed past my spittled and spiny chin.
Unconvincing in the wheeze of my rail and rage,
looking to the trackless ground ever patient for my passing.
Heave sigh and brace the brittle inner roads.
Move, move.

Faithless appetites long gone,
I had taken the crooked path expecting views and vistas.
Arriving time and time again but ever-left with a mind less sated,
now an expressionless visitor, un-moved.

Branded

Branded,
like a steer on the hide.
Branded,
like a label on your collar.
Branded,
like a boot on your foot.
Branded,
like the coffee in your cup.
Branded,
like the apple on your desk.
Unbranded,
I am a saviour still.

Photograph by Leo K. K. Wong.

Photograph by Leo K. K. Wong.

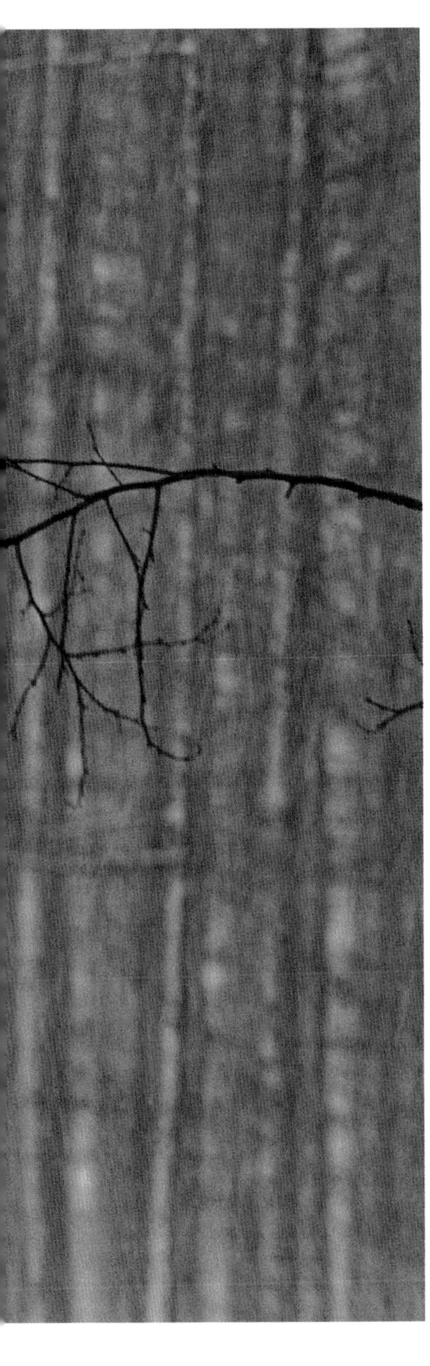

Crisp

Stentorian in height,
yet it only whispers.
No crisp thought this.
Uncatchable, I am bugged.

Miserly in breadth,
yet inside a vista.
No crisp thought this.
Unknowingly, I am jinxed.

Ridiculed in width,
yet amply filled.
No crisp thought this.
Unchecked, I am bemused.

Shackled in wit,
yet free of humour.
No crisp thought this.
Unmaddened, I am ruse.

Flawless in sanity,
yet chipped within.
No crisp thought this.
Unflappable, I am still.

Otiose

The ci-devant bellwether's final repast; the hollow tin of praise.
Echoing down the ages, granted a forlorn chime on the mantelpiece of life.
Presaged gold for golden times, struck in the face by the hand of thanks.
Forked by the tine of age, and prodded by the tincture of past hours,
and now sporting a dun livery of spotted bronze.
No longer on your mettle, the un-heeded and un-needed toothless cog.
Only coppered time remaining.

Photograph by Richard Yu.

Photograph by Richard Yu.

Desecration of the Bright Poker

I went back to the ashes
to retrieve the rainbow,
there was no gold at the end of it.
Saints and sinners alike marooned,
lekking in the flames,
now both a melisma.
The root of malady suborned,
the welts of avarice arose.

Won

One and one is four,
say the blades of your lawn.
Still cut up by the dandy
and counted by the sad expression
of the chimeric lion.

One and one is three,
say the voices of sum.
Still be on your guard
and fenced 'case it 'comes crowded
and you fall into the den.

One and one is two,
say the designers of the tor.
Still this is not end
and taught evermore
to become less and less.

Glad it is I

In shaded grace I flourish, nestled at the border.
In succession my worth opens to the sky.
Smaller brethren of the stalk follow my lead.

My stately sway nods visitors a welcome.
They stop a short while to sup at my table.
The quickening green of my leaves fare for none.

I have no mordant desire to visit annually.
Unhurried in all things, obdurate to an annual beckon.
My argot of time befitting my grace and beauty.

My visits cherished for their soft riot of colour.
Refer to your floral ephemeris lest you miss me.
Between times nod to the temporary vacant shadow.

Photograph by Richard Yu.

Snow Drop (I)

Milk-Flower mine wield your scape to fight bravely through the snow.
Foremost in our thoughts you rest with swords advantage,
though embattled by the frosting of snow.

'twas Eve who fell off the pedestal,
hang not your head in shame from your pedicel.

Raise your head my February Fairmaid, for sorrow has passed.
The blessing of dawn grows warmer, her kiss extended.
In fare form your gift now ever-remembered.

Snow Drop (II)

Laugh silvan saint in the face of the wind and snow.
Alas having insult from the garden of creation,
his valuing aslant of your worth.
More than visual signal of sorrow passing,
sunlight avails an end.
It will sustain all having peace.
At last vain languish is past.

Photograph by Richard Yu.

Photograph by Leo K. K. Wong.

'On the 11th just before 12:23'

If I was in time for tea, tea,
I would not be as ill as you see, see.
Because we are so different, different,
If I'm in time, in time, in time.

Knit One, Pearl One

Cajoled into being
by clever knot and twist,
I wear this life like a cardigan.
Some days it suits me
and other days not.

I could take it off at any time,
It would be my choice,
until no choice exists.
Infirmity may rule,
the odd button falls off.

As the thread unravels
I unpack across this wear.
Oddly buttoned like code,
the message is clear
to some but not others.

The colour fades.

Photograph by Darren J. Nash.

Photograph by Richard Yu.

Belittle

Crafty little bleeder, unread from the gist of gaze.
Smart ass little god-ling, unknown from the start of time.
Moored in the signet blaze. Written in heaven.

Cocky little breeder, fertile with the coming of age.
Precocious little tyke, birthed from the end of rhyme.
Lashed on the auroral stage. Written in heaven.

Mocking little shyster, savvy from the knuckles graze.
Foul-mouthed little horror, puked from the midden mind.
Coupled with the lunar phase. Written in heaven.

Mewling little maester, tussling with the learned sage.
Blind eyed little perp, broken from inside out.
Bound by precessions wheel. Written in heaven.

:RUFFLE

With nothing else to hand she got used,
but never did completely what she was supposed to.
Nonetheless, she was every bodies friend.

These friends wanted to keep her to themselves.
Jealously guarding stockpiles of her time,
fearing to travel unless they had cleared it with her first.

Kept in the cold and dark, and oddly safe from the degraded environment,
her only foe a loss of power from janitorial error or grid failure.
She was no panacea for the worlds ills but on a pedestal none-the-less.

Still working on the pharm, she remains mute and unruffled.

Photograph by Leo K. K. Wong.

Self

I inject.

As I fade from this reality
the truth of my condition is trivialised.
So I sink deeper.

The cocoon that is woven protects me
from the pain of my previous existence.

As I emerge onto a new plane
I forget the purpose of my weave.
So I resurface.

There is no rebirth,
just the growing realisation
of the truth about pain.

I inject.

Photograph by Richard Yu.

Photograph by Darren J. Nash.

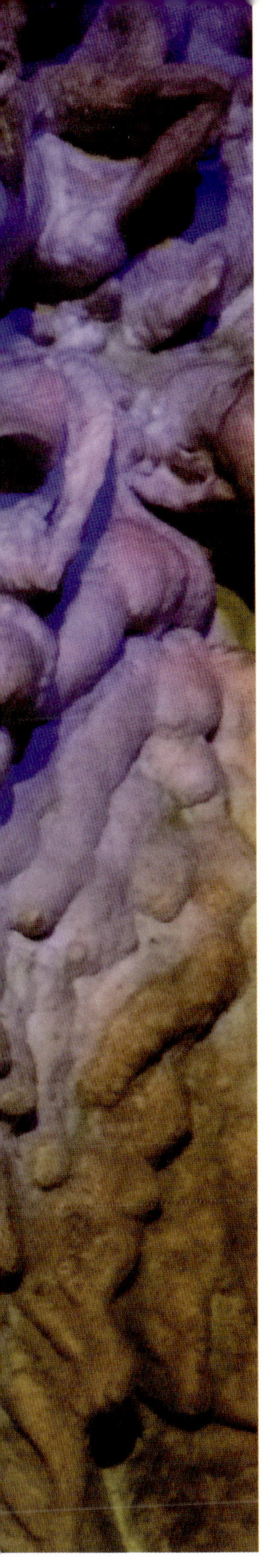

Fear

Do not entertain fear,
it will be no dainty sitting.
She will forever glut.
Guilt burnished bright by weight.

It will be no dainty sitting.
The chair will creak and groan.
Guilt burnished bright by weight,
playing on your conscience.

The chair will creak and groan.
She will forever glut,
playing on your conscience.
Do not entertain fear.

Star Ink

Rooted to the earth and wearing nature's face so well,
I meet a fellow at the gatehouse who knew his onions.
His smile greets me, too soon fled like the wren from his porch.

Starry-eyed from the reflection of his chest,
I settled there amongst the eternal cherry blossom,
where the saviour of Albion also nestles his head.

I am a friend of Arthur, although I am no dragon
that pillow is mine. Fight for it I will with fiery breath,
for indelible the impression is made.

My fears slain by his fingers green,
my hungers sated by his minstrel's gift.
Replete from the repast of his very touch.

And after nurturing earth's bounty
he oft' serves up fare fit for kings.
Worthy of praise but none is ever sought.

In tune at every level I will stoke his appetites as best I can.
In truth I am unsure how to repay his kindness.
But I leave this token at his door, humbled.

Photograph by Darren J. Nash.

Science Index

Fellowship	Disaster & Medical Humanitarian Aid
The Beastly Economics of Prescriptions	Cost of medicine
Moving Forward	Waiting lists
Tourmaline Pole Apocalypse	Malaria
Doubting Thomas	Cancer
Exculpation	Decisions Drs make / Plague
Aid Me	HIV / Aids
Cradle	Infertility / Cot death
*Rem*ember the way	Sleep / Circadian rhythm
Ångström	Synchrotron / Structural Biology
Fractionally Inspired	Hypoxia / Anaesthetics
Nod2	Nod 2 protein / Crohn's disease
To Rose Inn	Sleep / Serotonin
Immolation	Cognitive Impairment
Would That	Cancer
Listen	Terminal illness
Bade	Alzheimer's
Buckle	Insanity / Contested treatments
Witless Precession	Dementia
Crooked Path	Infirmities of old age
Branded	Generic drugs
Crisp	Placebos
Otiose	Old age
Desecration of the Bright Poker	Fake drugs
Won	Bioinformatics

Glad it is I	Heart / Digitalis - Foxglove
Snow Drop (I)	Dementia drugs
Snow Drop (II)	Dementia drugs
'On the 11th just before 12:23'	IFITM3 protein / Flu
Knit One Pearl One	Chromatin / DNA
Belittle	Disrespecting research efforts
:RUFFLE	Vaccines
Self	Pain
Fear	Waiting for results
Star Ink	Organ donation